Growing Up Depressed

Mackenzie

DORRANCE
PUBLISHING CO
EST. 1920
PITTSBURGH, PENNSYLVANIA 15238

Dorrance Publishing Co
585 Alpha Drive, Suite 103
Pittsburgh, PA 15238
Visit our website at *www.dorrancebookstore.com*

ISBN: 978-1-6470-2565-6
eISBN: 978-1-6470-2644-8

to my 'forever and always,' without you, this would not be possible

Contents

Voices In My Head

An earthquake has erupted
Inside of my chest

Feels like I've been holding
My breath for a month
With no rest

Each waking moment
I am put to the test

If you really want
To enter my head
Please be my guest

There's a path of perfection
With helping hands
That offer assistance

I walk in reverse
Down an alley
With valor and persistence

Tears rush in

With no delay

Thinking of everything and nothing

As I lay

Hiding from Heaven

And its rays

Everyone's open

With nothing to say

As I go through another box of tissues

As tears consume the day

The real me knows what's wrong
And what's right

Yet when it comes time to speak
The voice always keeps quiet

The left convinces me of whatever it wants
Until I buy it

The right showers love
And I choose to deny it

My two sides are talking
But it feels more like a riot

A majority of my thoughts
Come at night
When I can't stop thinking

And when I wanna feel my ego
I can't seem to stop drinking

I pray the Lord my soul to keep
I close my eyes
I still can't sleep

My mind is racing
My mind is spinning
I think of what it'd be like
To have a new beginning

Sleep to me
Means little to nothing
My thoughts are loud
They might actually mean something

I like being alone
But I hate myself
I hate my thoughts
But I love self doubts

A thousand different thoughts
But I never know what to say
A thousand different voices
Talk to me throughout the day

I'm unable to recognize myself
Not only in the mirror
But through other people as well

To me this only confirms one thing
I do not love
A single
Soul

Because to love another soul
Is to recognize
Yourself in another person

My expenses are high

I don't have much to show

Deep down I have

Much to say

It will be

The ones who love me most

Who will

Be the ones that pay

I have to go party

So I don't seem antisocial

I just want to feel accepted

Source of happiness needs to be corrected

While my mind is always neglected

Antisocial may be

Lonely at times

But it makes

Me feel safe

While I'm barely alive

I could ramble
For 127 hours
Before someone summons
The nerve to cut me off

I know my self defense
Will reject their help
With a scoff

I can see in
Their heart they have
Something important to say

But when they leave
So does the color in my eyes
Turning them back to grey

I only enjoy events when I black out

Because I don't want

My mind to remember

That I'm always

Longing for togetherness

Like it's Christmas time in December

Alone or blending in

I don't know what's better

They say cover your scars

But it's to them that I tether

Got rid of all my poisons
So my mind could declutter
I couldn't act
Couldn't think
And my speech was
But a stutter

My body is frozen
I can't seem to function
When I try to live sober
My life begins to malfunction

As soon as they're in my system
I remember why
The feeling's so addicting
As soon as it wears off
Tears fill my eyes
My throat begins restricting

I hear two voices
Speaking
And a lab coat says it's
A mental disorder

Which explains why
I'm tweaking
Accumulate prescriptions
Like a hoarder

It explains why
I lay alone praying
For anything on earth
To make my life shorter

Always tired
Always gone
Always lonely
When I'm alone

My body needs movement
It can't ever stop
Or the pressure of my thoughts
Will make my head pop

Don't stop doing
Sleep makes me weak
Nothing to say
But still my mouth speaks

A twelve hour work day
Is better than fifteen minutes solo
My mind never stops moving
And it always drags me so low

If life is but a story

And it's my own that I write

Why do I go back and forth

And debate on what's right

To me life doesn't seem like a story

But more like a fight

I exhaust myself trying to see

If the end is in sight

Until then I'll find my comfort

In the shadows of the night

People always ask
What goes on in your head
How do I explain to them
I think I'd be better off dead

Life is a gift
Ask and it is given
I could achieve so much
If I could escape from my own mental prison

Blades stacked high
And permanently stained with red
My bloodstream is trapped
In a cycle of never ending meds

As the door closes
Tears flow 'til I have no vision
Do you think anyone will notice
My brand new incision

Ego takes over
I forget what I said
No matter the weather
I can't ever move outside my bed

Try to fuse happiness
Instead I get fission
If it's such a good thing
Why is it such a hard decision

Put their hands around me for comfort

Now my head's riled

Every day's a fight to survive

Like I'm living in the wild

'Til I'm six feet deep

I'll label my condition mild

My opinion may change

When my parents have to bury

Their own child

A heart that beats
With each passing
Season
A body tied to it
That moves with no rhyme or
Reason

I tried to change
But pain is a go to
Compromise
If I really went away
It would come as no
Surprise

Besides death
What stops a heart quicker
Than despair in a mother's
Eyes

I joke and banter
To say I'm dramatic
I pretend that my mind's not
A cluttered attic

Really I'm crying and dying
For help
When it's just me
I don't completely trust myself

I wish they could hear me
I feel like I'm screaming
I'm calm for a moment
I realize I'm dreaming

If we're placing bets

On my odds

I'd guess they're about

One in a million

They think

I've got a chance

I might make it

I'll be free

But

I see the

Things that they

Don't see

I fear this evil in me

Might be permanently embedded

It feels wrong that I'm

The first one who said it

I am the way I am

My parents don't deserve the credit

I hate the way I am

I wish I could make some edits

Ask me how I'm feeling

Don't you people understand

I stopped to look at myself in the mirror

And I wish I would've ran

Layer after layer

Of continuous failure

Treat my body terribly

I hate my behavior

As I begin to inspect

This constant disrespect

I try to correct

And it becomes so depleting

And it keeps on repeating

I'm getting too tired

To keep on competing

Unnecessary unhappiness
That's what he diagnoses me with
My unhappiness is who I am
And I don't want to change it
Saying it's unnecessary
Makes me only want to quit

They label me unnecessary
My will to live is arbitrary
That concept is kind of scary
My joy inside is momentary
Try to blend in so I'm ordinary
My sins leave me unsanitary
Drown in my insanity
Reassured by the fact that my time here
Is ultimately only temporary

You know you

Could

Be happy

If

You just

Gave it some effort

Yes

I'm aware

I like it

My way

It's a choice

I'll live with forever

Many others think
They know me
No one understands
Like you do

The mask is
What they see
But the darkness
That's for you

Over everything else
You have precedence
You take control
And I reminisce

As I look back in time
You've always been present
If you're so easy to leave
Why do you always come back

Deep in my thoughts
It's you I resent
You stole so much
And it's strength that I lack

A feeling

An emotion

A spark

A smile

These things for me

I have not had

In awhile

I'm desperate

I'm longing

To feel just about anything

This state that I'm in

Is continually crushing

But a blade's end

Is sharp

And my skin

Still soft

And as blood pours out

Something finally seeps in

A feeling

An emotion

A spark

A smile

I lay awake each night

And I pray with my eyes wide open

I pray they don't come back

To terrorize

To haunt

To destroy me from the inside

But each night I fall

And each night they come back

Howling like dogs

Prowling the city

Roaming until they've fed

Growling until they get their fill

Around my chest
It has a tight grip
We're right at the edge
And I just might slip

I hear everything and nothing
All at the same time
I know it comes from evil
But the power so divine

Eyes are stressed
Now filled with terror
For now they know
I'm not their wearer

I have a thousand words
That now remain hidden
My throat begins to close
And my breath is forbidden

Losing everything
I feel my body and mind part
I brace myself
It's now about to start

Sympathy is only
Growing colder
Condition grows worse
As I get older

A trait I hate
But I still accept it
A muse I use
Getting hard now to quit

Your love
Your expression
Both things I can hear
But I feel next to nothing
When you show me your real tears

Sorrow fills my heart
My spirit broken
My mind implodes
From words unspoken
My tears fill pools
For me to soak in
My heart a void
Filled up with sin
Not a soul can help
No peer no kin

What's worse than a
Soul full of sadness
Or a mind full of madness

Living in a sane world as a psycho
Covering as a person that I don't know
Smile and laugh to complete the show

Right now I feel like I'm in
A state of acting psychotic
Light in the distance
And it's almost exotic

Nothing's worse than a life's tale

Not told truthfully

Self destruction that's completed

Each day ruthlessly

I have my noose tied

But it still lays on my neck loosely

I look in the mirror

And see

The greatest work of art

A feeling

I've always longed

To grasp

Even just for

A moment

Instead

I look down in the void

And see

The greatest work of art

It doesn't

Feel

Right

What I'm doing

To my

Body

Mind

And soul

But then again

A lot of

Things

Don't feel right

Anymore

I try to give her up
I really do
But the only time I feel alive is when I use

Float in and out of consciousness
Sobriety feels acidic
Something about a daze
Feels oddly therapeutic

Comforting to know
That she'll always be there
And it's calming seeing her
Float through the air

Fireworks explode
The moment our mouths meet
But when I get back to Earth
Harsh reality greets

Half a day drifts away
And I'm already longing
So easy to miss her
She gives me belonging

Everything I am

Is

Nothing at all

Materials do

A decent job

Defining

Pictures bring

Back

Painful reminding

Toxins are

Excellent at

Refining

Actions and intentions

Are simply not

Aligning

You say

Run away

And I stare eye to eye

He says

Ask me more

And I don't push and pry

She looks at my life

And laughs with scorn

Outside face stable

But inside I mourn

They look right through

When it's my face they see

One thing they

Don't care for at all

Me

Living in a world

Where

I live

To go to bed

The noise

Pounding in my head

Spreads

Throughout my face

Arms

Legs

Stomach

Soul

This noise

Silence

I hate the silence

I hear

When I'm alone

Covers me like a tarp

Eats me alive

Like bacteria

Who knew

Something so quiet

Could ring

So loud

And cause such hysteria

Out on my own

Like a bird flown from a nest

I embrace sunshine on my face

And wind in my back

Confident I will prevail

This time I think it's true

I smile

I laugh

At all things anew

Dark cloud rolls north

Nothing too large it seems

One raindrop on my head

A thread of hair is all it touches

Yet that's all it took

One trigger

To evoke a storm much bigger

First drops fall by the dozen

The hundreds

And now there are thousands

I'm covered in rain drops

I'm torn by sharp rocks

I'll continue crying

Until all my tears stop

I can't speak

I can't write

I can't move

I can't fight

Everything and anything

I feel no affection

Everything and anything

I feel no connection

Room is damp
Hands are cuffed
Body weak
Mouth is stuffed

Bruises plenty
Evil lives in me rent free
No matter the season
Or what's meant to be
The evil will always stay
Right there waiting for me

Let me go
So I can leave you behind
Lines are always blurred
But you're a clear sign
Present and future daunting
I wish I could rewind
One look through this lens
You'd see my heart confined

For this reason the ties between us ought to be snapped
You think I'm content but my heart has collapsed
Taking control without consent is all that you grasp
I live in shades of grey and blue
Everything I had I gave to you

You stole my childhood with my optimistic vision
Mind body heart are always in collision
All of us together are confined to this prison

Please let me go so I can
Leave you in the past
With you I cannot move
Body stuck in a cast
And when you're on your way
I can finally relax

1-800-273-8255

2
People that reside in my cage
One sweet and youth-infused
The other boils in rage

7
Reminds me of the luck I live off
I see so many at the top
While I'm stuck in the trough

3
A perfect number for a group of friends close-knit
I surround myself with bodies
But the emotions never legit

8
Arms wrap my body up
Removing life from me slowly
Like a suction cup

2
A pair
A loved one to hold
I have a heart of dust and want one of gold

5
Fingers so dainty
With so much power
Conduct the visions of my plan to live my last hour

5
Seconds to make this call and now my life saved
I want to be different
Change the way I behave

A look in my eyes

See my world's demise

A smile used to be my prize

Now my smile's a disguise

I live to get high

Wish I lived in the sky

Happiness comes as a surprise

Happiness is only filled with lies

Hate the road I'm on
Yet I keep my foot on the pedal
Stuck on the gas
And my toes are made of metal

Highway to Hell would be better
Than where I'm going
I'm destined for somewhere deeper
And my anticipation is growing

No bends no twists no turns
No speed limit either
I look back at the grass
And it sure looks greener

I am beyond fixable

I am beyond a mess

Nothing to live for

Yet

I am beyond stressed

A complex indulgence in pain

As if it were candy

Self destructive person

And

It is beyond handy

I make it easy to hate

And harder to sympathize

You'd think making the same mistake

Would

Make me

Beyond wise

This moment
I know I could
Make it
Last forever

If I could only
Find the
Courage
To actually
Pull the trigger

To separate the
Spirit from the body
The peaceful
From the haughty
And leave my lessons
For those
Foolish enough
To worship my
Transgressions

Should I tell them
Nobody is home
Because everybody's
Knocking

I see them
They can't see me
Like a ghost
In the shade
The day
I make it back
History will be made

I miss being home
And the
Warmth that it brings
Right now
I belong outside
Even though it still stings

Be honest
Have you ever really wondered
What it'd feel like
To not be alive

Seriously thought about
What would happen
If your existence
Came to an end

At first it makes you
Uneasy and it makes
Your mind bend

Then after real consideration
I wouldn't mind
Leaving my generation

At first they might hurt
It might turn their
Faith rotten

After full moons come and go
I'll be like the rest
Of them
Forgotten

Cloak of oppression

Is the only article wearable

No matter who I speak to

My journey doesn't feel comparable

I do not learn

Even after living through the parable

My shell is frail and worn

So easily tearable

For the sake of my future generations

I pray this gene isn't shareable

Body's up
But my eyes are tired
Time for sleep
But my brain is wired

Thoughts tell me
I'm living for nothing
No matter the number of times I hear it
The feeling's still crushing

My mind is splattered paint on a wall

And it's messy as shit

I'm only organized when I take my whiskey neat

When I pass out is when I quit

I'll forget everything just for the night

Impaired is my sight

Beat to a pulp is my might

Positivity seems right

But the taste of it makes my jaw tight

They say my future's bright

I should be thankful but I take it as spite

If I only had an hour

To live

Sixty minutes

Left in this dimension

And every one of my

Choices was at my retention

I would spend my time the same

Battling my other half in a ruthless contention

They say they love me

They say they care

They say I'm unique

That no other compares

But what would they say

And what would they mention

If for the last thirty-six hundred seconds

My neck has been broken

As I hang from suspension

An hour apart

Is an hour in the dark

Yet an hour together

Feels all the same

The only difference

Is the feeling you give my pain

In the dark

I'm confronted

And paralyzed in fear

Together

Brings smiles for a minute

Then you start to shift my gears

You bring a slow

And dull pain

Which I guess I can prefer

In the dark

I'm all alone

And right from wrong begins to blur

My head and
My heart
Just aren't in sync
Wish I could start
Acting right
Before I start to sink
Wish I could control
The thoughts
I think

My heart wants love
That's stubborn
As hell
My mind convinces
Me
I ought to burn there instead
Better off
My soul dead
Than tying any
Emotional threads

I wish I could let you in

For a minute

For a moment

I think it would scare you

To see a person so broken

I know you fear darkness

I know you fear solitary

I know to you

These feelings seem arbitrary

I have no control

Please tell me you relate

I know you're not like me

You don't have this trait

Do not miss me

Do not be filled with sorrow

We both know what I am

What I am is poison

An anchor of tomorrow

Leave me with the others

In the shadows

In the past

Make my face a forgotten memory

If you're going to rank me with the others

Please rank me last

Difficult to envision what's next

For the upcoming year

When the past continuously

Whispers in my ear

This makes it easy to live

A life controlled by fear

All good things are invisible

They're nowhere near

A future doesn't seem relevant

Something I don't have to plan for

So there it sits

Unaccounted for

But fast approaching

To an unopened door

My future's knocking

I don't want it anymore

So I'll just sit here waiting for nothing

Glued to the boards of the floor

Way deep down
I know
I am not capable
Of change

My dreams
Lurk and linger
But stay just out of range

They speak
From the shadows
And lay in the dark

Any light I get
Is their cue
To spark

To my brother

It's required I be an example

I'd show him what life

Provides is ample

I do right

In his sight

Prove that despite

My path not very bright

You can still take flight

On my lip I bite

Knowing the facade

I applaud

Knowing I've been broken

When I've spoken

Words of encouragement when my mind's deranged

Preaching joy when it's long been estranged

I don't like mirrors

Or any reflections

I wish the light

Would shine in a different direction

I wish I had the means

For cosmetic correction

So I could stare in his eyes

And not fret any inspection

So I could live without fear of

Constant human rejection

It's crazy that two

Quick injections

Could cure all

Broken sections

Until then and despite

Your objection

I'll stay staring

And hating my own complexion

Love

A state of mind
I want
To be in
But can a person in Hell
Have the state of mind
That belongs in Heaven

Thoughts

Thoughts

Thoughts

Swirl and run

Sometimes it's torture

Sometimes it's fun

I think and I think

Until my head melts

Around me they sympathize

And I know it's heartfelt

I sit back and admire

The hand I was dealt

Based on my coordinates

I know I'm covered in wealth

But no dollar amount

Could cure my health

I wish things
Had the ability
To set my soul on fire
Instead the flames
Burn up my chest

I wish I was like them
I wish I had
Set passions and desires
Instead the past
Clutters the present
I love and hate the mess

I imagine what it's like
To wake up and love
The air that fills the soul

I envision living in
Sunshine and warmth freely
And not buried in the cold

My dreams are like pyrite
They shine and they glitter
But they still aren't gold

You say you want
Me to talk
To understand
My mind
While writing
Each thought I give
On paper perfectly
Lined

But I'm not sure
Where to
Start describing
This endless
Void

I have irrational fears
I know
And you know
What will make
Me feel
Safer

No prescription will
Ever be enough
No antidepressant
No opioid

You text me one sentence

And that might as well be

My life sentence

I read and reread

A thousand times plus one

Think and rethink

What you meant when

You sent those nine words

Could it be my chance

For repentance

Or maybe you didn't really mean anything

When you sent this

The number of different

Scenarios you can

Think of I thought

Of a hundred more

I read so far into

Those words

Now I'm trapped

In a different

Dimension

Why do I

Always overthink

Every human

Connection

On the days that I'm up

I can see the vision so clearly

I see myself so powerful

The darkness actually fears me

I cherish these days

I know they'll only last a moment

It won't be long before

I belong to the hold of mental torment

Don't speak a word

To me

Not one sentence

Not one phrase

Can't you tell I'm

In a state of paralysis

Based on this gaze

Nothing is really

Wrong in real life

That's not the case

Yet I'm addicted to tragedy

And it's deception

That I chase

I formulate some demons

And lock them up

In a maze

Every now and then

I meet an angel reaching out

Our fingertips hardly graze

Telling me that millions

Of people

Are experiencing the

Same thing

As me

Doesn't take away any

Of the sickness

A thought should be simple

Something that just passes through the head

A thought should not be

A component constantly compounding

And putting pressure on the skull

An overworked anomaly resting

On the occipital making sight dull

This thought in my hands

That I hold and let hover

That consumes but I don't

Want a soul to discover

It started small and now

My whole life it covers

Why do I do this

Why do I obsess

Why is my life picture perfect

And I insist on making it a mess

Look at this line of thoughts

That only wanted to pass by

Without their weight

I swear I could fly

Real talk
Dark thoughts

With all the hatred that
Fills my body
With lack of care for
Any commodity
If it wasn't for my family
If it wasn't for my kin
By age fourteen I feel
As if I would've already
Committed the suicidal sin

I got younger siblings

They're supposed to want to

Be like me

But I wouldn't wish

That on anyone

Not even

My worst enemy

Nineteen times around the sun

Nineteen years of fake fun

Almost two decades I hid my secrets

Behind anger I tried to be strong

And the overbearing stress

Went on much too long

I tried to set a good example

And provide a clear path

But I burned everything I saw

With this torturous wrath

I hold so much guilt

Knowing the idol I've built

For the many others that turn to me

When there was indecision

I acted as if my intentions

Were based on careful precision

Behind closed doors

I admire my incisions

Clear thoughts and a smile

Two things I thought only I was missing

Years later I've learned my admirers

Have similar dark visions

I try so very hard
To keep my thoughts
To a minimal

The number of thoughts
That pass through is so overbearing
It turns my soul clinical

I look deep in my parent's eyes

And my heart nearly collapses

As I know with all their energy they're caring

When they look in my eyes

Their hearts nearly break

As they realize my soul's barren

How do you

Help someone

Want to

Help themselves

Do you know what it's like
Having a voice in your head
It makes me psychologically crazy

Do you know how much
Pain I have hidden
An amount that even amazes me

I see my future ahead
And it's just out of reach

You'd think I'd learn from my mistakes
But even trauma can't teach

People always ask me so much shit

What's my deal

What's my life

Why did I give it up and quit

In my opinion they should be asking

How I feel deep down

How my head's in the stars but feet

Are stuck on the ground

How I'm screaming but my lips

Somehow never make a sound

But people don't care when you show

Them your heart

You give it to them whole and they

Return it in parts

I close my eyes

The room spins faster

And faster

I think of my life

And I think of

Disaster

I put too much stress

On my dinner plate

I think I'll only be loved

If I grow up to be great

I think it's better

To hide my mental state

Than to look at the people I've locked out

And let them through the gate

Do not try to talk to me

I'll only fuck it up

I'd rather start off honest

And nip this in the bud

Than let you enter my world

And drag you through the mud

So when you see me just walk on by

And let me sink deeper into this rut

I'm buried deep

So I send out a lifeline

When someone responds

I ignore and let my pulse flatline

Some of you look at my life

And gaze at the divine

Few choose to look deeper

At the parts that don't shine

Act like I live on the sun

When in actuality I sleep on the moon

They see all that I've built

And don't recognize all that's in ruin

I glisten like I've been in paradise

And every day is an emotional monsoon

This act gets difficult to perfect

I wouldn't mind if it ended soon

But the end is hard to see

And it's nowhere near

I honestly can't remember the last time

I felt my head was clear

No one to blame not even my guidance

Because we see two different things when looking in the mirror

Through their eyes a perfect creation

Through mine there's only fear

I wait and wait
On a hand to be extended
For cuts to be mended
For dreams apprehended

Once it comes my heart skips
I feel a glimpse of hope
But nope
I revert to how I'll always cope

Alone in my basement
Filled with nothing but cement
Upset for no reason
Regardless of the season
Denying any loving guidance
I've never been the same since
That first time I tripped up
And my body was ripped up
Years go by I'm still the same
I've survived a lot while being insane

My ideal alternate reality

Is one filled with demons and brutality

Where sin is a normality

In my alternate reality

I'm just another detainee

Death being the only guarantee

Lucifer holds the master key

To the beloved olive tree

That I so badly wanna see

But unfortunately

He has no sympathy

For someone guilty of murder in the first degree

Controlled by a rage in my soul

I realized I had to grow up fast

I thought it was temporary

I didn't think it would last

Mom raised me right

Tried to rid off any doubt

For years I've been trapped in the dark

And still can't get out

I know I had to live
I had to make it
Through the day

Thinking of reasons to live
But I don't really know
What to say

Ask me if I'm free to talk
I honestly wish that I wasn't
Ask me how many problems
I can easily list a dozen
Ask me if the cold bothers me
In all truth it doesn't

Don't try to help me

No

I don't need that energy

I'd rather drown myself

In Crown and some Hennessy

You try to pull me up

But down is where I'm

Meant to be

They want me to share all my feelings

I laugh at a statement so amusing

If I started sharing real thoughts

It'd really get confusing

I'd share how I have so much

But always feel like I'm losing

How I was raised with love

But I still have a problem using

How I need so much help

But it's always help I'm refusing

Even though I feel it's hopeless

It's still happiness I'm pursuing

I have a lot of blame to give

The person in the mirror I'm accusing

My parents say they're

Proud of me

But they don't know

The half of me

I wonder if they saw

All sides of me

Would they still think

The best of me

Words fill up my mouth

And never pour out

It leaves me asphyxiated

And struggling to call out

Phrases fall out in texts

And are regretted later

The anger towards myself

Burns hotter than the equator

I have a sense I'd be okay

If I was turned to dust

In my right mind

I realize that statement is actually specious

Relationship with Lucifer

Is one built on lust

All the darkness that surrounds

Is what completes us

When no one else

Wants to keep us

We fly high above

So no one can see us

Descriptions of this life

I keep light and facetious

Deep in my heart

I want this bond to rust

And just disappear

And turn to dust

She wants a look in my thoughts

Too bad they're demonic

She acts like my illness is curable

So unfortunate it's chronic

She thinks I'm changing permanently

Almost humorous it's only periodic

Week after week

I'll sit in this chair

I'll shed my tears

To show I may care

I leave and I'm numb

Can't change something already bare

Writing you all a letter

But I can't manage any words to find

How does one describe a crippled will to live

To a group of people so kind

As words start to form sentences

So do the tears in my eyes

Maybe the fact that I'm crying

Should lead me to revise

And reconsider my decision

To take a human breath

To realize I'm being selfish

Determining the time of my own death

What makes a broken soul

Want to cry

What makes a youthful energy

Cripple and die

No matter the time

I search and pry

I always find my thoughts

Consumed by degrading lies

I need to blink a few times
Just to make sure
I can still see straight

Tears blur my vision
I fear the time for change
Is too late

I cry too often
For someone who's
Barely an adult

I have no one to blame
This life
Is all my fault

Sometimes when I sit still for a few hours
I start to have crazy thoughts
I start to think no one loves me
I start to think about the future

During these points I feel something
Deeper than hopeless
I feel more than just a mess
But all the feelings I take them and store them away
Naive enough to believe they won't reappear another day

I hate company but being alone is quite terrifying
Therapy's a waste of money
Nothing is ever clarifying
I sit and think of ways to end everything
From pills to car crashes to my neck wrapped in string

This is why I shouldn't be left alone
I look at old pictures and how my face shone
Now I look into my own vacant eyes
What used to be joy now feels like a disguise

I wonder if something's
Broken inside me that'll
Never be able to be fixed

How sad it would be
To be sad for the
Remainder of my days

I wonder if a person
Can really change or if
Deep down they'll
Always be the same

If so
I'm doomed for years
And at this point
I can finally accept it

I thought it was only me

I thought I was alone

I figured I was too in debt

To ever repay this loan

A room full of people similar to me

And we're striving for something more

Although we can't quite label it

In the meantime we'll just use metaphors

Even when I'm happy
I don't know
If I'm happy

I overthink all my emotions
But especially the good ones

Maybe deep down I'm
Afraid of pure bliss
Even scarier
Maybe deep down I'm
Not capable of pure bliss

Tell me I'm unique
And that I can make a difference
To me this seems
Like quite a bold inference

You see my multiple personalities
And say I have hidden abilities
You say you can look past my transgressions
That I'm more than just my depression

I'm not sure if you're insane
Or if I can give you my belief
I'm not sure if I'm ready to be happy
And not live in grief

I cry myself to sleep

And I wake up tired

I hate all of me and

The way my brain's wired

I don't know why I'm sad

Or why I act this way

They tell me the world's colorful

But I see the world in shades of grey

They see me fighting

And they give their utmost respect

What they don't seem to notice

Is the apparent disconnect

Between what's needed

And the wanted pain I protect

If I could put all the fears together

For you to collect

You could take a look into my world

And yours would be wrecked

When I'm hurt

I hurt deeply

And cover it

Quite discreetly

My wounds should

Be a secret

Can't let go of emotions

So I keep it

Why can't I ever let

Anything go

Every day I'm alive

I'm putting on a show

They say a picture is worth
A thousand words
But this one
Left me speechless

I find myself paralyzed
Holding a photo
Of a girl with such
Eager and sweetness

Wonder and confusion
Begin to fill
How has such strength
Turned into such weakness

I ask over and over
And when I try to explain
I'm devastated
To find myself speechless

I'm always tired

Yet never can sleep

I walk through my day

As if I were asleep

Brain talks all hours

Mouth never makes a peep

I can feel it coming

As signs begin to creep

Pressure begins to build

Through the cracks it seeps

It has pushed me to the edge

The time has come to leap

When I sit here in the dark
And abuse my meds
When I lay awake
Crying in bed
I look at the day before me
And only feel dread

When I examine
My life ahead
I should feel joy
But instead
I see a virus
That won't stop until it embeds

I define life by my disabilities

Anorexic and dyslectic

Numb yet still eclectic

Depression brought on by anxiety

Discovered drugs now I struggle with sobriety

Passion fueled by rage

Shy but want to be on stage

Too broken for my age

Can't go an afternoon without smoking

Think that I'm okay by the way that I'm joking

Get love from other people's temporary intimacy

The love for myself is still lost at sea

Ever since I can remember

My smile's been fake

I look at pictures of myself

And my false face of joy

I feel sorrow for the soul

Behind the camera

Thinking I'm smiling because I want to

I'm only smiling so my

Numbness won't haunt you

I think of how

I can't remember

Any good childhood memories

It's simply disheartening

I think of how

Mom and Dad

Couldn't fix me

Despite their strong partnering

I think of how

I look at

All things

With a vision so darkening

Turn up my music
So I can drown out
My dark thoughts

Close my eyes and
Sink deep enough
So I can see spots

No matter what I try
No matter the amount I lie
My brain gives the same reply

Dark thoughts
That make me so demonic
Covered with a smile
My ways so sporadic

Fuck you and the

Happiness you hold

Fuck your ability to

Shine and be bold

Fuck me and all

My jealousy

Fuck being sober

And pass the Hennessy

Fuck being alive when

I know I'm crazy

Fuck some clear vision

I'd rather be hazy

Sitting with a knife in my hand

And thoughts so unpleasant

My will to live

Thinner than the moon at crescent

Because of my actions

I'm told to take an antidepressant

I stare at my palm

The pill looking so pleasant

I begin to flash back

To days before adolescence

Back to days when the mind

Was free and effervescent

Back to days when the smile

Shone brighter than fluorescent

Maybe I can change again

Bring back a soul incandescent

Maybe I can be anti depressed

If I take my antidepressants

Don't you ever fear
You'll die if you
Do this too often

Isn't it hard being
So difficult when it'd be
Easier to soften

It's okay if I pass
I can't turn around
I belong in a coffin

You can't do anything right

You can't live off the dreams you write

You have too many emotions

And not enough devotions

You long for love

But hate the face in the mirror

You don't look in her eyes

Because deep down you fear her

You can't do it

You should quit

Get rid of hopes and dreams

Take in all the madness

Black out anything that gleams

How do you feel today

What a laughable question
If you know the quest I'm on
You know it's fueled by aggression
I know it feels like compression
Each time I enter a session
When I talk about the digression
Of my self progression
It feels like this may be my best confession
But the longer this depression
Remains in my possession
My greatest obsession
Is the tally of my transgressions

I'm not okay

But thank you for asking

I can survive but

Not thrive

I'm no good at multitasking

I'm living

Each day

Just to go to bed

The only thing

I look forward to

Is sleep

When I finally

Get there I think

Of how I've wasted time

Then I cry

My eyes dry

Until I fall asleep

I'm too tired

To do anything

My life is exhausting

Even though I'm moving

I can't seem to feel a thing

Even though I'm breathing

Each breath I take in stings

And when my face begins to shine

My mood soon after swings

I am by myself
Art trapped inside a shell
If you ask me where I'm at my best
Come visit me in hell
Not a single wish came true
Despite throwing coins in the well

I couldn't find real love
Even if I had a magnifying glass
Love happiness joy
Are concepts I can't seem to grasp

Bipolar depression's something real
Sometimes I just can't seem to feel
I hold down all my anger until it breaks the seal

Close relationships cause me stress
At my age I still don't know a loving caress
Is it safe to show my feelings
Even if I am a mess
Trust puts my mind to the test
Ask my loved ones they can attest
I feel like when I'm manic
Is when I'm at my best

I look back and still feel the emotions

That I felt in that moment

The horror of waking up

The day filled with mental torment

I'd like to say I've moved past

And that I've grown

But no one could believe me

Based on the dismal progress I've shown

I'm told each day

Should be viewed like it's a gift

I tell myself it's okay

If my death appears swift

Without it

I fear I'm nothing special

I begin to doubt

My own credentials

The path I'm on

Is not sequential

The thoughts I have

Far from prudential

No way I'll reach

My full potential

I seek the end
I want to die
And that's not to say
I have not tried

I've consumed until
My mind stopped working
Then drove for miles
With memory searching

I've mixed this and that
Without further examination
Each time arriving safely
My mind left on vacation

Just two milligrams
The dosage considered lethal
I doubled it and still made it
To praise the Sunday steeple

Maybe I am meant for more
Because death I seem to miss
I come so close and am left stranded
The taste barely reaching my lips

I've been hopeless so long

I forgot what it's like

To sit in peace and enjoy life's song

When asked what makes me smile I can't answer honestly

This life I have is permanent

And that's how it seems meant to be

Outsiders are confused and ask what I worry about
That's a loaded question so I'll start with my self doubt
I ponder if I've let down the ones that I love
Not just the ones breathing but the ones that watch from above

I feel guilty because I know people look to me for guidance
I give the best advice but a talk for myself is filled with silence
I know I'm not that happy and I feel others can see right through me
I wish when my loved ones died of overdoses it would finally get through to me

The list is too long for aspects that bring forth anxiety
I fear those I hold close only lie to me
I toss and turn at night because I'm not who I say I am
That I'm closer to dying than a sacrificial lamb

I cry rivers believing God's dead and there is no peace
I worry I'll always chase bliss and never get a piece
I could go on and on about the stresses in my life
It's too hard holding all this pain inside so I turn to the knife

Never thought unspoken words

Could be so prominent

Never thought regret

Would be so dominant

Never thought insecurity

Could walk around so confident

I wish my family didn't have to deal

Just to get by

I wish when I reminisced on the past

My heart wouldn't cry

I wish I lived a life full of stories true

And not packed with lies

I wish when I was happy

It didn't take me by surprise

I wish I was fine

I wish I could let go

I wish I knew where to draw the line

I wish time would move slow

I wish my angels were on Earth

I wish I had more to show

I wished for a lot

And that's not how I planned it

If I could take one wish

And have the Creator grant it

It'd be an explanation

As to why I was born on this planet

Every once in awhile
The voices stop
My head is filled with silence

These moments offer
Just as much suffering
And just as much violence

Maybe these moments
Are meant for
Learning and guidance

When I am up

I'm really high

There's no stopping my potential

But when I am down

I fall so low

The world moves fast

But my thoughts move slow

I wish someone could answer

As to why I'm so unpredictable

I wish I could replace my thoughts

With something more permissible

I've been crying all night
Do you think anyone
Will notice

A better question might be
How do I learn how to
Control this

I forgot what it felt like

To feel absolutely nothing

To wake up at one a.m.

Because my thoughts won't stop rushing

I forgot what it felt like

When food no longer has taste

To look at a full plate

And let it go to waste

Who can identify my pain

Who can stop this train

Who can explain

The thunder and the rain

There's something in the air

That spreads and leaves me bare

I inhale with no care

My functions now impair

Another night
Separating abuse
Into different compartments
Another night
Sitting on my bed
In my broken apartment

I disappear
I fade away
My breath leaves
As my body lay
I float up
And see my skin grey
I awake
Like a rose in May
Despair fills me up
I realize I'm okay

I find myself

Sleepwalking

I try to figure where I'm headed

But it's hard to tell

Next thing you know

I'm sleepwalking

And I'm on my way to hell

People Leave Too Soon

That's okay that you are missing

That's okay that you're at rest

It only makes me dizzy

And feel like I'm a mess

Always hearing that I'm blessed

In the background there's screaming stress

They say it's okay

Because you're finally at peace

The second your breath ceased

Unfortunate I own this life

And it's not just a lease

Swipe to give you a call

My breath begins to stall

Another painful reminder

My eyes begin to ball

I get in my feelings

So often because

All my idols have passed

And when I'm alone

Those thoughts attack me

I feel harassed

But I still listen

And now

My feelings are masked

They say just be happy

And I try to

So they don't ask

Really I'd rather be alone

In the dark

With my ghosts

And a full flask

Tough knowing you're not here anymore

Even tougher remembering it

Each day things feel as if they're the same

But when moments come

Where I recognize you're only a memory

I start to feel the pain

I would kill for a second in your presence

Who knows what I'd do for a hug

I cling onto that fantasy

Like an addict to a drug

I long for an embrace

I long to see your face

My last words to you I wish I could trace

And replace them with something better

Something meaningful

Something special

My last words to you I hate

As they cause a mind so stressful

I hate the fact that I can't recall

Our last hug

Our last laugh

Our last phone call

My head starts to crack

Knowing I can't remember

Your last I love you to the moon and back

For the first time

In a long time

I saw myself inside your eyes

Not in happiness this time

But in your pain

In your numbness

In your sorrow

I saw me

I saw you

And I understood you

For the first time in a long time

I handle death irrationally

Increased anxiety

Bearing on me

I didn't plan it

And I can't stand it

A soul taken from me by a bandit

I never got to say goodbye

Tears ran out and my eyes are dry

Smile is gone and replaced by sighs

All I am is now sadness or anger

I put myself knowingly in the way of danger

I look at pictures of myself

And see the face of a stranger

I stand and I socialize

In a room packed with

People who are

Second best to you at the most

I talk and I get bored

The only thing

I long for

Is to again see your ghost

At night I can't sleep

As I toss and turn

My mind can't comprehend

My heroes' ashes now rest in an urn

Sometimes it fuels a fire

Of devastating rage

Sometimes tears fall as I

Read your words on a page

It's not fair

On our last call

I never got to say goodbye

I've been crying so long my

Mouth's gone dry

But the one aspect that digs

Deep and hurts the most

Is knowing you're no longer human

And now you're a ghost

So many loved ones have passed

And I've began to lose count

Part of me gone

The voices no longer make a sound

As my memories fade

So does the joy in my heart

I wish I could've gone with

When it was your time to depart

I miss you

But at least we have those memories

I hate the part of you

That fucked up my psychology

I belittle the people who say

Certain things are just meant to be

Now that I don't have you in my life

I'm not stable mentally

I forgot how much I missed you

After I read your old poems

I realize we weren't too different

Based on the pain in your words

I notice I took advantage of your heart

And the amount that you loved

What's the point of all these prayers
If they can't bring you back
What's the point of these meds
If I still get panic attacks

Why am I living a life
That you're not in
Why am I trying to live
Despite all this sin

Can't Survive Without It

I enjoy your company
Even though I wish I could
Run from me

And no matter the number of you
I choose to attach to
It's always lonesomeness that
I seem to attract to

The only thing I remember
About last night
Is that I was trying to
Drink my problems away

When will I learn
That it never quite
Works that way

I've learned a lot
From drinking until
I pass out
I've learned that despite
The amount I consume
I cannot wipe this pain out

I wake up
I feel just the same as before
Tears make me weak
And leave my eyes sore

I should give up drinking
And let go of its power
But what else can take the
Pain away for a few hours

I don't want
A prescription
I'd rather do it on my own

Anxiety medication
Is the reason
Part of my family can't come home

I know they're destroying me
But I can't break my bad habits
Everything I want
Sits right in front of my eyes
But I can't bring myself to grab it
I'm too afraid of success
And what I'll do when I have it
So I'll settle in self pity
And self label myself an addict

Mind's running

And I can't relax

Without my daily dose

Of illegal Xanax

This is how

I fill my cracks

Consuming darkness

Like it's a snack

Looking for help but they've

All turned their backs

So bliss takes a back seat

In my mental annex

While I slip away

Thank goodness for Xanax

It took me awhile
But I finally got it figured
I found out why I'm addicted
And what gets my mind so triggered

Without a single substance
My mind never stops talking
It causes temptation to stay near
Always lurking always stalking

Each night that I cave
I choose a different melody
Soon I hear those voices I miss
And they take away my memory

I need my medicine

So my head will

Shut the fuck up

All talk

All worry

Without it I'll blow up

I need my high

So my blood

Won't burn up

Reliance isn't fading

My will

Far from grownup

I miss drugs

And I fucking hate it when I'm sober

I count down my sobriety

And celebrate when it's over

Because I only ever commit short term

And never for a lifetime

When I'm close to the end

These substances have always

Been my lifeline

You may find that depressing

I've learned to just accept it

But every time I relapse

Deep down I always regret it

They ask me what my

Greatest fear is

I worry it's my addiction

Something that's

In my control is the greatest

Cause of my affliction

I'm meant for nothing

A thought that's always been

My greatest conviction

How ironic the same statement

Is the source

Of my greatest restriction

Don't you ever wonder
What caused such
Deep rooted addiction

I ponder this and a lot more
Growing more accustomed
To my inflictions

I know myself and
I know that I'm sad
I still post like I'm living
Now I'm pissed off and mad
But who can I blame but
The face in my reflection
Speaking of
I hate when
A mirror's in my direction
At first
I reasoned this could
Get fixed with foreign alcohol
Then it got out of control
When I was taking Fentanyl
After each and every party
I sink even further
Look back at my younger self
And cry knowing I hurt her

You can decide

If I live or die

You can decide

If I smile or cry

You can decide

Because you're my supply

You can decide

Because without you I'm dry

I wonder if my friends
Would still befriend me
If they knew what I was

Would they give me their time
Knowing if I take it I
Have to be buzzed

My love for them is at the minimum
Narcissistic addict
Is me as a synonym

I wonder why I make things
More difficult by putting
Up a front

I don't try to feel alive
Knowing my existence will
Be blunt

They think they know me
But I feel differently
I have too many addictions
Maybe death is meant to be

I don't care about the amount
Of love you sent to me
No amount of anything
Will ever make a dent in me

Going through a phase where
Without you I'm confident
It seems when you're not with me
I don't get as many compliments

I try to comprehend
What it'd feel like
To trust a true friend
Someone solid that won't bend
Even when exposed to a heart
That cannot seem to mend

I look into the Devil's eyes

And I caught him winking

Because we both know

No matter what I show

I can't go a night without drinking

I know you read that

And you're probably thinking

If I have some self control

I could stop sinking

I love and hate

The way my life is

I love the pain

And what the knife gives

But I hate the way

I feel at the end of the day

The feeling of being

Worthless

The feeling of sinking below

The surface

It's only 5 p.m.
And I'm already
Seeing double

The amount of
Alcohol in my blood
Is putting me in trouble

I tell others
I drink for fun

I tell myself
I drink so I pass out
And don't grab the gun

I go to take another drink

And now I'm feeling dizzy

I look back at the old me

I admit I start to miss me

I'm slow moving

And there's nothing

I love more

Than to starve myself

For hours on end

Just to feel it burn my core

I'm not good with words
When I try to speak I stutter
Seems like when I'm with you
Is the only time I declutter

Even though you're no good
I'll always reach for your hand
You feel so perfect at first
Long term you leave me sinking in quicksand

I thought I had recovered
It felt like the real thing
I was married to this idea
I even bought a ring
I guess in the end
To addiction I'll always cling

I'm running out of ways
To hurt my own body
My tolerance is so high
I'm starting to feel godly

I'm running out of ways
To forget my past
My high is short-lived
My high doesn't last

I'm running out of ways
To not feel a thing
Sadness creeps in
And that shit always stings

These pills go down easier
Than water on a hot afternoon
They hit my bloodstream
Pupils the size of a full moon

But do you expect me
To give a fuck
When I would rather
Spend a buck
On something that'll
Take my head way up

When gravity kicks in
I'm coming down
And my two feet
Kiss the ground
My head starts to pound
My mouth doesn't make a sound

I hate the concrete
I'd rather walk on air
I hate everyone
And their nerve to care
About a person so broken
With a soul so bare

My friends frustrate me
They don't understand
The drugs are calling
I need to meet their demand

I gotta smile
When I'm struggling to stand
I can't catch my breath
When I'm living on land

If God is really real
And this is His master creation
I'd really hate
To see my life at completion

I can't imagine a future
At all
Much less one with a
Smile on my face

I sit here alone
And I think of
All the memories
Mistakes
And misfortunes I'd
Like to erase

A secret life

It's a small miracle I'm alive

Fueled by the dark energy

That I inject to survive

A pool full of liquor

Head first I dive

The amount means nothing

I'll always survive

I'm riding shotgun going 90

While Hades drives

I look forward to

The day I arrive

The underworld might be

The only place I can thrive

I think
I have a problem

One of the main reasons
I'm waking up

Is living to
Cover the space memories are taking up

One eye closed just so I can

Concentrate

I realize two of everything isn't normal

Now I'm trying to consolidate

All feelings

All intentions

Are things I cover and

Would rather not mention

Every single drop

I can't let any go to waste

When it's all inside

Is when I finally gain some space

And put some distance

Between my thoughts and reality

The line starts to blur

Between living and tragedy

It's time for more
Self inflicted pain
I know I'll later regret it

This disease grows
Day by day
It now feels permanently embedded

Flashing lights
And provocative sights
More lefts than rights
On this Saturday night

I almost had it
But then I lost it
Almost grabbed it
But I dropped it

I could almost see
I was almost free
I was almost me
I could almost be

But then I gave into
The threat
I guess to this day
That is my greatest regret

When I walk with the clouds

The voices aren't so loud

I wander away from the crowd

Even though I'm solo now

My actions still don't make me proud

One taste of you after
Two months sober
That's all it took

You taste different this time but
You're still hitting hard
And leaving me shook

You knew one taste
Is all it would take
To lock me down again

Now you've got me prisoner
And everybody knows
Chains don't bend

This feeling it gives
Spreads from my
Head to my toes

This feeling I feel
I don't really
Know

That's what's exciting
And frightening
Altogether

That's what changes
My mood quicker
Than the Midwest weather

I wake up and I'm soaring

I know

This will only last a minute

But I'm going to stay

Here and dream

While I'm in it

I know the neurons my

Brain's composed of

Might have taken a divet

But we have billions of those

So this damage I

Can live with

My loved ones see
The bright-eyed
Blonde-haired child
I used to be

They adore that
Version of my past
And I can't help
But agree

They give all
That they can
And smother me with hugs

But that birthday money
They gave me
I use to buy drugs

Nothing at first
But then
I feel guilt

Would they still
Adore me
Knowing
This is what was built

I made this drink

Way too strong

And it's been way too long

Since I had a sober thought

Surrounded by this

Dream-like song

Trying my best to

Fit in and belong

Usually when I think I'm right

I end up wrong

All that ambition

I once had is gone

A bottle of vodka

In less than three hours

This liquid in my bloodstream

Gives me magical powers

It feels so refreshing

Finally my head is clear

I can't wait

The end might be finally near

The room spins

As I try to get locked in

Juice and gin

Is my secret win

A smile emerges

Adrenaline surges

It's too hard to quit

These everlasting urges

These voices speaking to me

Are my personal scourges

As I sit here in bliss
Even now you're
Easy to miss

Under further inspection
There's a quite simple
Detection

I'm missing you for
All the reasons
I shouldn't be

I miss the way you
Put a cloak over
My humility

The way you make happy feel
Like something I could be
But I can only get it through you
Because you hold the key

Reasons I love you

I've got a million and five

Reason number one

You give me a reason to be alive

When you're inside me

My body finally warms up

The only time I smile

When you fill my cup

At first you were the cure

To my depression

Now I'm a different person with you

Controlled by aggression

Sometimes

The truth

Is hard

To

Swallow

It

Goes down

Easier

With a

Spoonful

Of sugar

And

A bottle

Of

Tequila

It came fast

And walked away even quicker

It felt like the real thing

Which makes me even sicker

My friends say I'm an alcoholic

But that's just not true

Only time I consume

Is to cover up feeling blue

Alcoholic but that's

Just a word they're saying

I only drink until I'm numb

A game I like playing

Alcoholic but they only see the surface

I only consume because I need it

Without it I have no purpose

Solution to this problem
Is to overmedicate
In my mind
These words simply resonate

Check a couple boxes
Now I have prescription pills
Overflow of chemicals
Creates a brand new thrill

When I want something extra
I turn to the street
My trust and my life
In the hands of strangers I meet

One at a time
That is not enough
I want to overdose
Will my Maker call my bluff

How much is too much
This I'll never know
You can see for yourself
What does the autopsy show

You say you'll accept me

For exactly who I am

But can you accept an alcoholic

Can you be with someone

Who's been proven

To be so toxic

To be honest

I only drink to black out

And to be honest

I only spend time with them for the clout

Deep down

I know this life is not what I'm about

To be honest

I drink and never lose my consciousness

And to be honest

Sometimes I wish I was born with less

Maybe then

My head wouldn't be such a mess

I build myself up

And convince my head

I'll only need you

One day a week

But let's be real

I'm much too weak

Fuck it

I need you every single day

I'm sober now is just

Something to say

And I never say what I

Actually mean

You help me blend in

To avoid being seen

Tired from crying

Feels like

I just took a Xanax

Even five of those beauties

Couldn't ease this head

To relax

I had everything and more

Just to let it

Slip through the cracks

Starved myself all day

Just so this liquor

Would burn my stomach

I start speaking of

My true feelings and

They tell me to change the subject

Finger down my throat

To try and clear my core

This can't be

What I'm living for

Surely I was created with

More in store

Everyone looks in my eyes

But they don't seem to see the gore

I love when I'm

Intoxicated

Life isn't so damn

Complicated

My thoughts are much more

Abbreviated

When my head's shut up and

Inebriated

The high's wearing off I'm feeling

Deflated

I want what I can't have now I'm

Frustrated

The moment I see it I'm immediately

Elated

Sober for a day I'd rather be

Serrated

Just another day
And it's just another drug
Just another day
For a hole to be dug
I'll sweep all this mess
Underneath the rug

Just another day
To mask the pain
Just a way
To cope with my brain
A way to make me
Feel not so insane

Just a voice in my head
That no one seems to notice
Just illegal Adderall
That continually helps me focus

Just another day
I realize I'm missing what I was
Just another reason
For me to catch a buzz

Bite my tongue
Just to swallow this liquor
I'd do just about anything
To make it absorb quicker
I'd drink even faster
If it didn't make me sicker
This gives me stability
When the light starts to flicker

By the 15th of October
I should be two months sober
If I could only withstand the
Longing
Calling
Shouting
Screaming
That my former companion
Still rings from high canyons

Every time our eyes click
I only focus on getting a hit
We go in knowing
That you're toxic to me
And for a moment time stops
When our energies meet
Without you I'm lost
With you I feel free

Yet I think we'd both confirm
You're a parasitic worm
Each time I think of you
My stomach starts to squirm

And I'll think of the 15th of October
If it's all that worth it
To try and stay sober

Under toxins
Two minds seem to speak louder

One tells me to push myself
Until I nearly crack

The other is gentle
And tells me to pull back

A will to listen and self respect
Are a couple things I lack

Because I often find myself pushing
Until I only see black

God Doesn't Feel Real

They say I look strong

But looks can be deceiving

I keep praying to God

Even though I've stopped believing

I'm fragile

Once you peel back the layers

I say He's fake

But get mad when He doesn't answer my prayers

I get angry

I yell at Christ

No answers come

And temptations suffice

Now I'm trapped

Between this vice

Living in peace

It must be nice

Walk through hell

I've done it twice

Paid with my soul

What a high price

To have just a piece

And just a slice

Of love to melt

This heart of ice

Perhaps I should ask for help

And swallow my pride

Maybe I should open up

So you can lead and guide

The distance between you and I

I fear is quite wide

But I know you'll take me in

Even though I'm filled with pride

I inked a cross on my wrist

To remind me of Life's gift

But now my thoughts are twisted

My beliefs have since shifted

I know my days are limited

Maybe more so than others

Because the path that I walk

Death always hovers

Each night under covers

I uncover my true fears

I don't fear I am worthless

With nothing to show

For this is a fact

I already know

I don't fear street drugs

Or marijuana laced with blow

For when I take them

It's the only time my world glows

I fear I'll keep going

And never give up

I fear I'll live for years

In a system corrupt

I fear I'll be alive

With no real purpose

I fear I'll never drown

Living life just barely above the surface

I drink myself numb

I am depressed

Too many drugs in one night

I am a mess

Spinning in slow motion

I need a rest

I cry to a stranger

Their words make me feel compressed

If God is real

I'll put Him to the test

I tried religion

But it gave me too much stress

They suggest therapy

I do not take requests

Maybe I am on Earth

For a specific reason

And maybe there's a

Point to me living

Maybe I'm actually not

Quite worthless

And maybe there might

Be a higher power

Because based on standard statistics

I should be incarcerated

Deformed

Or lying dead waiting

For a stranger to find me

Come the morning hour

Through my trials
Denials
And deep thoughts that stretch for miles

You stay confusing me
Amusing me
Now you're losing me

I don't know your purpose
Your meaning
Your expectations

However you've left me sinking
Struggling
And unamused

I don't know who you are
But I have a feeling
We will meet soon

Smile's fake
But the pain is real
Talk to God
But I've taken Satan's deal
Preach self love
But I find I skip meals

Body's out of place and so is my mind
Looking forward yet still stuck in rewind
Can't talk can't scream
My neck's in a bind

Self harm just to feel like I'm still here
Hate what I see when I look in the mirror
Ingest this and that to try and think clearer

Wrote my goodbyes a long time ago
No friends just foes
That's the way my life always goes

If God is real
Why am I suffering this much
If the Word is so moving
Why can't I feel its touch
They say use Jesus to lean on
As your crutch

They say the way I am now
Prevents me from being a believer
My old ways and habits
Need to be cut off with a cleaver

I don't feel like this is real
And the facts seem fake
I listened to the rules
And I don't know how much I can take

No faith in anything
But I still send
Prayers to God

To ask for a sign
A symbol
A line

So I can finally confirm
That I'm on the wrong path
He never responds
But yet I still ask
To heal the destruction
Of the depressing aftermath

Everything Will Be Okay

I know you can beat this

Although it won't be done with ease

But that feeling when you're finally free

Will have you embracing Life's gentle breeze

Some days you'll bump into old ways

They'll force you to stumble

But you're stronger now

You'll get back running

This time you will not crumble

I've said all I can say

About the feeling of moral decay

Sometimes the old feelings

Start to weigh

But healing starts now

No need for delay

Right now happens once

No chance for replays

When darkness starts to knock

Remember it's okay to not be okay

Turn to your god

Fold your hands and start to pray

Because you were put on this Earth

To be more than prey

You were built for love

Feel it in your airway

You were built to shine

Alongside the sun's rays

You're capable of anything

When you get out of your own way

You are so powerful

No limits to what you can convey